IPHONE XS

USER GUIDE

FOR **NEWCOMERS**

Complete iOS 12 guide
for beginners and seniors

Stephen W. Rock

Dedicated to all my readers

Acknowledgement

Ii want to say a very big thank you to Michael Lime, a 3D builder, my colleague. He gave me moral support throughout the process of writing this book.

Table of Contents

Introduction 8

Chapter 1...9

The iPhone XS 9

Chapter 2..12

Secure Your iPhone With Face ID 12

Setting up Face ID 12

Using the Face ID 13

How To Charge iPhone Wirelessly. 13

Charging wirelessly 14

Chapter 3..16

Tips and Tricks for the iPhone XS..................16

Using The Portrait Mode..............................17

Control Depth..18

Use The Memoji. 19

Become Skilled At Using Gestures 20

Enable Do Not Disturb. 21

Bring back the home button 22

Taking A Screenshot. 23

Enable True Tone. 24

Face ID Security. 25

Enable Siri on the iPhone XS 26

Video Quality Like No Other 27

Utilize Group FaceTime 28

Make Use Of One-Handed Mode. 29

Split The Screen's View 30

Turning Phone Off. 31

Set Up Apple Pay. 32

Access To Notification Center 33

Force Closing Apps 34

Customizing The Control Center 35

Chapter 4. 36

How To Use Apple Pay 36

Setting Up The Apple Pay. 36

Using The Apple Pay. 37

Chapter 5. 38

Tips for using iOS 12 effectively 38

Saving Your Passwords. 39

Ability To Turn On 'Do Not Disturb' During Bedtime. ... 40

Measuring Objects With An App. 41

Insert Siri shortcuts 42

Track your screen time 43

Place Limits on apps.................................44

Easy Force Closing apps. 45

Chapter 6...46

How To Use Siri On Your Iphone....................46

How to invoke Siri 46

How to type and ask Siri 48

Tips To Ensure That Siri Serves You Well 49

Chapter 7...52

How To Maintain Your iPhone 52

Chapter 8...56

Prolonging Your iPhones Battery Life. 56

Disclaimer...59

About the author 60

Introduction

The title of this book already gives a hint on what the book is about. It is a guide for new users of the iPhone XS.

There are about eight detailed chapters in the book. Dividing the whole book into three parts, the first part introduces you into how to explore the iPhone XS, the middle exposes a comprehensive list of tricks and how to execute them, while the last part culminates with useful maintenance tips, including battery and overall iPhone.

Also, with the comprehensive list of commands, you'll definitely learn to be a pro in using Siri, Apple's voice assistant. You'll be a pro in using Apple Pay. You'll be an iOS 12 pro. Yes, an iOS 12 pro.

Now, start savoring the content of this book.

Chapter 1

The iPhone XS

Launched on September 28 2018, the iPhone XS is said by some to be the perfectly sized iPhone. With 5.8 inches, it's made of excellent-quality material. A glance at the phone and there's no doubting its elegance. With iPhones, you always expect a new upgrade and iPhone XS is no different. You'll find an improvements from the iPhone X.

With the camera, you still get the same dual-camera 12mp lens with f/24 aperture. But something noteworthy is that the image sensor is larger now. Might seem like nothing but wait till you're in low light and you'll be thankful for the enormous sensor size. It's also said that that iPhone XS has a better stereo than iPhone X.

Another area in which the iPhone XS is better than iPhone X is this feature of the camera called Smart HDR. What this does is that when you hit the shutter button, it takes the picture at 3 exposures. It then blends them all together to create the perfect photo. The reason it does this is to lighten very dark areas and darken very light areas.

There's this mind-blowing upgrade the iPhone XS also received. It's called Depth Control. What it does is it allows you to tweak the blur on a Portrait mode photo. You can increase the intensity of the blur or reduce it to any level you want. This is really cool, who doesn't like to be able to design exactly how he wants his pictures to look like.

Let's move to battery life. It is said that the iPhone XS battery can last up to a full day. Well it's got a 2658mAh Li-ion battery which is lesser than iPhone X 2716mAh so you shouldn't expect much. But there was a testing that showed that the screen can be kept on for 6 hours with heavy usage. Like watching videos, streaming music, using hefty apps in the background.

Well as with storage, iPhone XS still beats iPhone X. Something with apple is that they don't provide a slot for microSD. So i guess as compensation they are offering a storage space higher than iPhone X 256GB. With iPhone XS, you have option to choose between the regular 256GB or 512GB. Though you'll have to pay extra for the 512GB, i think it's worth it.

Just like its predecessor, iPhone XS comes with 2436 x 1125 pixels, Hexa Core and 64 GB storage. But hold on here comes the fun part. iPhone XS is equipped with v12.o iOS unlike iPhone X with v11.0.1. It's got a superb 4GB RAM a lot better than iPhone X 3GB with a A12 Bionic chip unlike iPhone X A11

Chapter 2

Secure Your iPhone With Face ID

Setting up Face ID

Before we set anything up, let's make sure there's nothing blocking your face or the phones TrueDepth camera. Try to keep the phone with arms length. And don't worry about contacts or glasses, Face ID can work with them.

To set it up,

1. Go to **Settings**
2. Choose **Face ID and Passcode**. Enter your passcode.
3. Select **Set up Face ID**
4. Put your phone in front of your face and hit **Get started.**
5. Make sure your face is in the frame. Move your head gently to complete the circle. When it's done, hit **Continue.**

6. You'll be asked to do it a second time. Do the same thing and click **Done**.

Using the Face ID

Tap to wake or raise to wake your phone. Hold it in portrait orientation and it should scan your face.
If you're in bright sunlight, you might want to bring the camera closer to your face.

Face ID has been tested to unlock even when you're wearing sunglasses, but not all. So if you're trying to unlock your phone but it isn't recognizing, pull the sunglass off.

How To Charge iPhone Wirelessly.

Later versions of iPhone (iPhone 8 and higher) have a glass back that enables Qi certified chargers to charge the phone wirelessly. There are many Qi certified chargers. But there are two which are Apple certified; Mophie and Belkin.

Charging wirelessly

To charge wirelessly, what you want to do is;
1. Plug your charger to the power. Be sure to use a power adapter that's recommended by the manufacturer.
2. Make sure to put your charger on a flat surface
3. Lay your iPhone in the middle of the charger with its screen facing upwards and your phone should start charging

That not all. Here are a few things to make to wireless charging run smoothly
- If vibration is turned on, your phone might very well move its position when it gets a notification as you're charging. Try to turn off vibration, at least when you charge
- Make sure your phone isn't connected to a USB when you're charging wirelessly, it won't charge.

- If your iPhone has a thick or magnetic case, remove it before charging. It might charge slowly or not at all.
- When charging, your phone might get somewhat hot. When it does, move it to a cooler environment.

Chapter 3

Tips and Tricks for the iPhone XS

Using The Portrait Mode

Using portrait mode with your iPhone XS is so smooth and it even gets better as you can use it with either the front-facing camera or the camera at the rear.

Using portrait mode is walk in the park. All you do is enter the **Camera app** and slide left on the menu slider and you should see **Portrait**.

From here you should see options of different lighting. Like Contour light, Natural light, Stage light and others. If you want to use the front camera in portrait mode, just hit the **rotate camera symbol** beside the **shutter icon**.

Control Depth.

The Depth Control option is very new to the iPhone world and of course you guessed right, iPhone XS has this feature. What Depth Control does is that it enables you be able to control the amount of blur that's in the background of the photo that has been taken.

To use this feature,
1. Enter **Photos**
2. Choose a portrait mode photo
3. Click **Edit**

You should see a slider down that allows you to manipulate the blur to how you want.

Use The Memoji.

With the previous iPhone X, apple gave us the ability to create Animojis . But with this iPhone XS, they are topping it a notch with a feature called **Memoji**. They are available on the iOS 12 of iPhone XS.

What a Memoji does is that it controls animated avatars using your facial expressions

To create a Memoji,

1. Open **Messages**
2. Click the **app drawer**
3. Select the **monkey symbol**.

From here on, you will be able to customize your Memoji to your desire. After customizing and you are okay with it, save it by hitting **Done** at the top of the display.

Become Skilled At Using Gestures

Who knows may be the iPhone X is your first iPhone that does not have a home button. But fear not, you can learn how to use cool gestures to get by.

One of the gestures you can use is the swiping down from the bottom of the screen. When you do this, you can switch between apps easily. By swiping up, you will be able to shut down apps that you don't need any more.

You can also swipe down from the top. From the center, swipe down and the notifications will open. The **Control panel** appears when you swipe down from the right.

Enable Do Not Disturb.

You might just want to block out the noise one day and silence all notifications and calls. At that moment, what you do is switch **Do Not Disturb** on. With **Do Not Disturb**, all notifications and calls are silent which is great as you can use it in the car so you don't get tempted to reply to a message. If you can't hear it, you can't answer it.

1. Go to **Settings**
2. Then **Do Not Disturb**
3. Toggle **Do Not Disturb** on

To still be able to receive calls from specific contacts, click the **Allow Calls From** and set your desired contact.

Bring back the home button

If you've just got the iPhone XS, I'm sure you've been wondering why on earth did they have to remove the home button. I've felt your pain but really you get used to it pretty quickly.

But if you are a diehard fan, I'm happy to tell you that there's a way you can get your home button back. Well of course not the physical hardware home button, I'm talking about the virtual one.

All you do is,
1. Go to **Settings**
2. Select **General**.
3. Tap **Accessibility**
4. Choose **Assistive Touch**

From here, you can specify shortcuts of single tap, long press.

Taking A Screenshot.

There's no home button and I'm sure you're used to clicking the home and power button to take screenshots. The question is; how is it possible to take screenshots now with no home button on the iPhone X?

It's fairly easy to do. All you do is hold down the power button and the home button immediately. An image should show up at the bottom of the screen at the left side. And you can also hear the screenshot sound.

Enable True Tone.

There's this feature that's available on the iPhone X iOS 12. It is the true tone. What true tone does is that it adapts the color brightness of the screen to match the surroundings where you are. This helps to reduce the strain effect it will have on your eyes.

You should have this setting enabled on your phone by default, so you don't have to worry about switching anything on. But just in case, this option is for some reason not activated or you switched it off by mistake, Just go to **Settings** then **Display And Brightness**.

Face ID Security

Previously the security we had on our iPhones was Touch ID and we thought apple really made it. But with iOS 12 they've gone further. We now have Face ID.

And as the name implies, Face ID is an authentication process that relies on the information of the face for security.

To set Face ID up,

7. Enter **Settings app**
8. Select **Face ID and Passcode**.
9. Enter passcode.
10. Choose **Set up Face ID**
11. Follow the prompts it gives you and allow your face to be in the frame. Tilt your head slowly to finish the circle.
12. You will have to do it again. Follow the same steps.

Enable Siri on the iPhone XS

You know Siri right? The helpful Apple virtual assistant that carries out tasks according to what you command it. One of the task you can delegate to Siri is 'What is the time in London now? And the ever wise assistant will answer you.

To set up Siri:
1. Enter your **Settings**
2. Select **Siri & Search**
3. Then **Listen For 'Hey Siri'**
4. After this, To call up Siri, just say "Hey Siri"

Video Quality Like No Other

The video quality of your iPhone is set to 1080p by default. But who cares about default. There's a way you can set your phone to shoot videos with super high quality. And by high quality, I mean 4k resolution at 60 Fps (frames per second), incredible right? That's four times that of 1080p, imagine how smooth that can get.

To switch to 4k from the default 1080p,
1. Enter **Settings**
2. Move down and select **camera**
3. Hit **Record video**
4. Choose **4k at 60 fps**

Utilize Group FaceTime

In your iPhone XS, you can engage in group FaceTime calls. The number of people you can engage in with ranges up to 32. To set up group session, open the FaceTime app and manually choose whoever you want to add.

In fact, you can try it on a group chat in imessage and begin a FaceTime group call.
To do this

1. Open the **chat**
2. Click the initials that's a top the chat window.
3. Tap the camera symbol.

As the group FaceTime calls proceed, you can even add Animojis or stickers

Make Use Of One-Handed Mode

The iPhone XS is undeniably large. And it can be a real pain trying to navigate to type a message through the whole screen with one hand. Apple provided an antidote; they call it the one handed keyboard mode.

This feature is really awesome. What it does is it squishes the whole key board to one side, either left or right. With is this it's much more easier typing messages with one hand.

Too let this feature be turned on all the time,

1. Go to **Settings**
2. Select **General**
3. Tap **keyboards**
4. Then **One-handed mode**
5. Choose between right or left.

But if don't want it to be on always, just click the emoji icon on the keyboard. Choose either left or right.

Split The Screen's View

So you've got this really big screen, it will be a big waste if you don't make use of it well. You can go on with the normal display of the phone or you could just split the screen. When you use the split view in your iPhone XS it makes you get an extra view of some apps

Using split view is easy. Just open an app or website that works with it and rotate your phone to landscape mode. Verify that rotation lock is off. If it is not, from the top right side of the screen, swipe down and unlock the rotation lock icon.

Turning Phone Off

We all know that the button at the side of the phone is usually the power button. Of course that's how it has always been. But not this time around with the iPhone XS. That button is the lock button. So a good question is; How do we turn our phones off then?

The answer is not far fetched. Just press and hold the **Volume down** button and the **Power button** immediately.
Wait a little and the slider to turn off should show.

Set Up Apple Pay

Do you know that you can leave your wallet at home and pay for items with your iPhone? Yeah and that's its only made possible with Apple pay. With it, you can pay for items.

To use it, you'll first insert a card to the wallet by,
1. Going to **Settings**
2. Selecting **Wallet and Apple pay**
3. Then **Apple Pay**

Before you can use it, you should first contact your bank. It's very easy to use Apple Pay once it is set. Quickly press the lock button twice (lock button at the ride side of the phone). Scan your face if you set Face ID so purchase can be approved.

Access To Notification Center

What's interesting about the notification center is that you have access to it anywhere, any time no matter what you're doing on your iPhone. Whether you're in an app or at homescreen or lockscreen

It's very easy to this. Just swipe down from the very top of the screen and the notification center should open. Though you want to be careful not to tap the right corner of the screen cause that's where the control center is

Force Closing Apps

If you close an app on your iPhone XS the app still runs in the background. Some apps still perform certain tasks even though it is the background. To stop this we can force close the apps.

To force close an app,

1. Swipe up from the bottom of the screen
2. Don't release your hand, hold it for a while.
3. Now a card should appear, swipe up the card of the app you want to force close.

It is said though that force closing apps tends to drain more battery.

Customizing The Control Center

Customizing the control center is a cool option. It makes it easier to reach for features that you tend to use more often. You don't have to go far. You can even remove the ones that you think you don't need.

To do this,
1. Go to the **Settings**
2. Tap **Control Center**
3. Select **Customize Control**

Now you can remove and add what shows up on the control center, just tap the green (+) button to add a feature. A cool feature that you might want to add is the Apple TV remote.

Chapter 4

How To Use Apple Pay

It is now ever easy to use Apple pay. It can even be done through the iMessage app. All you do to activate is place the top of your phone near the **NFC** card terminal while putting your finger on the iPhone's sensor for Touch ID. But to be able to perform all these wonders, you've got set Apple pay up first.

Setting Up The Apple Pay

1. Open **Wallet**
2. Select **Add Credit or Debit card**.
3. Put your card details. Your card will now be verified with your bank
4. Once that is done, you are able to use Apple Pay.

Using The Apple Pay.

1. Put your phone near the card reader and what will appear on the screen should be the image of your card.
2. If you use Touch ID, Place your finger on the Touch ID sensor. Once your fingerprint is confirmed, you're golden.

If you want another card, press the one that is on the screen and select a different card. Real simple, uh?

However if your phone uses Face ID like iPhone X and higher, the process is a little different. It's not hard though. You just click twice on the side button. Then put your face to the camera so it can scan your face. After this, you simply hold the phone toward the card reader. Double click the side button again, if you want to use another card and just select a different card.

Chapter 5

Tips for using iOS 12 effectively

Saving Your Passwords

In the iOS 12 there a totally cool feature that helps users be able to follow up on their passwords. The new iOS is armed with a feature called **AutoFill Passwords**. This is usually kept in the iCloud keychain.

With this, you can add your own username and passwords from your **Settings app** to set for only some apps and websites. This feature will fill in your information automatically for you once you use Face ID or Touch ID after it identifies the ones that are logged

Ability To Turn On 'Do Not Disturb' During Bedtime.

The **Do Not Disturb** option got totally revamped in the iOS 12. With its extra feature, you are able to customize it more to suit your taste. Not only can you state clearly what times you want **Do Not Disturb** to be on at day, you can even set it to Bedtime mode.

If you set it, this will quiet down all the notifications all the way till the morning. To let you know that it the feature is set, the screen will display just the date and time and become dim.

Measuring Objects With An App.

Using the camera of your iPhone, iOS 12 allows you to measure objects with AR. When you use the measure app, you'll be able to measure different objects.

All you do is,

1. Open the **Measure app**.
2. Fix your iPhone's camera on the object to measure
3. Follow the guides it gives to line up your phone correctly.
4. Next, to view the measurements, you just click the display

Every display will always show the option to switch form inches to centimeters. Of course it doesn't give an accurate measurement like a hardware tape rule, it is really handy if you just want to take a quick measurement of an item.

Insert Siri shortcuts

There's a new advancement with Siri in the iOS 12. It's the option to add immediate actions and shortcut to Siri. Thought this option is still in beta for now and you can't do plenty with it, there are still some perks you can enjoy.

Like how you can set a voice commands so that Siri can do some specific tasks. Example, **View New photos.**
If you want to set a voice command'
1. Enter your **Settings**.
2. Selects **Siri and Search**
3. Click **My Shortcuts**

Once that is open you will be able select anyone that Siri suggests.

Track your screen time

In the iOS 12, apple is trying to urge us to use our phones lesser so we can have time for other important activities. There's this new feature, **Screen time**.

Screen time is an opportunity for you to set Downtime, check your phone usage and find out which apps are really eating away your time. When you use down time, you are able to put away your phone by restraining some applications from forwarding notifications.

Place Limits on apps

This is also one of the perks of screen time. It enables you to set app limits. This will enable you to reduce the time you spend on certain apps. You will be able to set how long the ban should last and for which days.

If you want to set app limits.
1. Fire up the **Settings app**
2. Move to **Screen time**
3. Then **App limits**. Select the groups of apps you want to set limit. Click the **Add**

Easy Force Closing apps.

With the iOS 12, the process of force closing apps is a lot simpler. Not only simpler also quicker. All you do is swipe up from the bottom of the display and just start swiping the apps you want to quit like that.

Y'know, previously force closing apps on phones without home button on previous iOS will have to take a longer method. You'll have to swipe up and hold down and wait before a minus sign will appear, then you now click

But now with newer phones like the iPhone XS and XS Max, they all have the iOS 12, so the process is a lot simpler.

Chapter 6

How To Use Siri On Your Iphone

Siri is the ever helpful apple voice assistant that you dish out commands to on your iPhone and it just it just carries it out for you.

But something to note is that there's not a specific app icon for Siri that you just tap and it open. So how then do you access Siri. For newer generations of iPhones, accessing Siri can be a little confusing even if you have been using previous versions of iPhone. All of that we will cover here

How to invoke Siri

By Clicking the home button or side button

On older versions of iPhone, pressing and holing the home button on your device will call up Siri. But on the iPhone X and higher, you summon Siri by pressing the button at the side of the phone.

By using the Bluetooth headset button.

If you use a headset that has remote, press and hold the button at the center and you should hear a ding.

By saying hey Siri

If your iPhone is iOS 8 or higher, you can summon Siri hands free by saying 'Hey Siri'. But you've got to first set it up.

1. Got to **Settings**
2. Choose **Siri & Search**
3. Enable **Listen For** 'Hey Siri' and obey the prompts it provides
4. From now you can summon Siri without having to press anything just say **"Hey Siri"**

What Can Siri do for you,

- Send messages for you
- Set a timer for you
- Play music
- Send tweets
- Check the weather
- Schedule events
- Send emails

- Calculate
- Find locations

Here are some things you can ask Siri

- 'Hey Siri, Set an alarm for 6 am'
- 'Hey Siri, What is the time New York?'
- 'Hey Siri, schedule a meeting with Sarah for Tuesday at 11oclock
- 'Hey Siri, how cold will it be today?'
- 'Hey Siri, remind me to do the dishes?'
- 'Hey Siri, play me Roar by Katy Perry'
- 'Hey Siri, call David Randall
- 'Hey Siri, open the Settings App'
- 'Hey Siri, how do I say hello in Spanish?'
- 'Hey Siri, who is the President of Iceland?'
- 'Hey Siri, turn off Bluetooth'

How to type and ask Siri

If you're the type that doesn't really fancy talking to Siri, you don't have to say something. You can just type your command. Though you'll have to set it up first

Here's how.

1. Enter **Settings**
2. Go to **General**
3. Select **Accessibility**
4. Move down to Siri and click the line
5. Switch on **Type To Siri**
6. The next time you activate Siri, all you do is type in your command

Tips To Ensure That Siri Serves You Well

While the apples virtual assistant is known for its top notch abilities, you may encounter some problems with it. Implement these few tips to allow Siri to better

Control how long Siri will listen

You have the power to control how long Siri will continue to encode your commands. You don't have to wait for it to recognize that you have stopped talking.

Just make sure that while you're asking your question or saying your command, you're holding down the power button

Alter Siri's language.
One of the key reasons why Siri may not understand your commands well can be because of your language. Even in English. Let's say you speak UK English. Siri may misinterpret your commands. So what you want to do is set the English to 'English (United Kingdom)

To adjust the language,
1. Enter the **Settings**
2. Go to **Siri and Search**
3. Select Language
4. Choose your desired language.

Having Smooth Data Connection

If you don't have data connection, Siri won't work. How Siri functions is that it records your voice and sends it to a server which converts your sayings and gives it back as text.

So if you're not connected to the internet, Siri is not going to work.

Changing Siri's gender
If you're a male and you prefer to have a male virtual brother around, you can switch the gender. Same goes for females.

Just,
1. Enter **Settings**
2. Then **Siri and Search**
3. Choose **Siri Voice**
4. Select your preferred voice.

Chapter 7

How To Maintain Your iPhone

We all know that iPhones are not biscuit change. They cost high. Well, they give superb quality so they are very well worth it. But such an investment will go to total waste if you don't take proper care of your treasure.

So here are some iOS maintenance tips for your consumption.

Put The Unwanted In The Garbage Truck

Do you remember that game that your buddy told you to try out and you felt it was total trash? Or yes, that app your neighbor introduced to you only for to find that it was a complete waste of time. Yes those applications. I'm pretty sure they are still sitting there in you app list

Throw them out and send them packing immediately. Not only do they use up the space of the phone, they also make it sluggish and your device slow. To delete an app, press and hold the app until it shakes like it's waving 'hey look at me' and delete or press the X at the corner.

Back Them Up

It's funny how many people do the bad stuff and only few do the good, like backing up your iPhones. You need to train yourself so that it becomes a habit.

Reason why backing up is so essential is because of this. Let's say your iPhone gets missing (I really hope that doesn't happen) or you there was a software update gone wrong or your device becomes faulty, retrieving your files will be almost impossible.

So don't wait for me, just back your phone up. You can back your phone up with iCloud or iTunes. In fact what's stopping you, just do both!

Update iOS

You be like 'Who needs an update. My iOS is just fine'. And I want you discard that feeling and throw it far away.

You need an update. With every new iOS there are fixes to bugs, updates for security, and brand new features and perks. You stick to your old iOS and it will be like you're living in the Stone Age.

What more, updating is like the easiest thing to do. Since we have OTA (Over The Air), updating iOS is just a matter of minutes.

To update,
1. Make sure to back up your phone as we warned earlier
2. Enter **Settings**
3. Then **General**
4. Then Choose **Software update**.
5. If an update is available, click **Download and install**.

Phone case and Screen protector

We all know how phone cases and screen protectors saves our lives every once in a while. Okay, not our life per say, it's our phones. Whenever your phone drops, a protective phone case will help to absorb the effect and shock of the fall.

And screens, oh screens are really special. And believe me when I say that you do not want them to break. So just buy a screen protector.

When you're purchasing either of the two, make sure it's of good quality and the design is what you desire.

Chapter 8

Prolonging Your iPhones Battery Life.

As with maintenance of phones, we all know how much battery means to us. Check out these tips to extend your phones battery life.

Forget Quitting Apps

You may probably be doing this, quitting apps regularly, I usually do so too in the past. But stop. you might think that you're saving you're battery, but actually you're degrading it.

In 2014, Apple explained to us that quitting apps sucks more battery as the next time you want to open the app, it will start all over again thereby, eating the batter.

Using The Auto Brightness Option.

Using full screen brightness sucks away your battery and I'm sure you know that. Unless you really need the extra brightness, don't be stubborn just use auto brightness.

This adjusts the screens brightness to the surroundings you're in.

Turn Low Power Mode On

Normally when you're phone reaches 20%, you'll be prompted to switch to low power mode. But you don't have to wait for your phone to urge you before you switch it. You can do it right after you finishing charging.

Low power mode stops all the background tasks and gives you more battery.

Turn Off Bluetooth.

It's not a new thing that putting your Bluetooth on regularly reduces the battery life. So if you're not using the Bluetooth, just put it off

Disclaimer

In as much as the author believes beginners will find this book helpful in learning how to use the iPhone XS, it is only a small book. It should not be relied upon solely for all iPhone tricks and troubleshooting.

About the author

Stephen Rock has been a certified apps developer and tech researcher for more than 12 years. Some of his 'how to' guides have appeared in a handful of international journals and tech blogs. He loves rabbits.

Facebook page @ Techgist

www.ingramcontent.com/pod-product-compliance
Lightning Source LLC
Chambersburg PA
CBHW031248050326
40690CB00007B/1005